What Every Child Should Know About
CLIMATE CHANGE

Children's Earth Sciences Books

BABY PROFESSOR

EDUCATION KIDS

Speedy Publishing LLC
40 E. Main St. #1156
Newark, DE 19711
www.speedypublishing.com

What is our climate? How is it changing? What does that mean for you and me? Read on and find out!

Coast of Antarctica. Glaciers and icebergs
of the Southern hemisphere.

THE CLIMATE IS CHANGING

The weather is what happens outside your window each day. The climate is the pattern of weather that happens over many days, months, and years over a particular area of the world. It may be raining or sunny today: that's the weather report. Knowing about our climate means we can know that our town has, on the average, so many inches of rain each year. We can even know with some confidence which months will be rainier and which will be drier.

People learn about the climate because a lot of what we do depends on our understanding it. You don't want to plant your seeds in a month that is usually so wet that the seeds will just drown or wash away. You don't want to be fooled by a warm spell and put away your winter coat if your knowledge of your climate tells you that more cold weather will probably show up soon.

Each part of the world has its own climate with its own specifics of temperature range, precipitation, and wind activity. But we all have one thing in common: all around our Earth, the climate is changing.

Icebergs of fantastic forms. Summer in Greenland.
Deep-water fjords of the Western coast.

WHY IS THE CLIMATE CHANGING?

At one level, the climate changing is nothing new. The whole Earth has gradually gotten warmer or colder, wetter or drier, over the centuries. Areas like North Africa, which are now broad desert, were once fertile lands with flowing rivers. During a period when the Earth's climate got a lot cooler, places where cities like London and New York now stand were deep under glaciers during an Ice Age.

Sometime a natural event, like a huge volcanic eruption throwing tons of dust and ash in the air, can cause the whole earth to cool so much for a few years that crops fail to grow and rivers freeze that never normally see ice. Read the Baby Professor book *What Happens Before and After Volcanoes Erupt?* to learn about this sort of natural event and climate change.

Water on arid soil.

But the climate change going on right now is different than anything the Earth has known before. It is caused by global warming: the Earth is getting warmer faster than at any time that scientists can find in its past.

Crater of Mount Bro-mo. Mount Bro-mo is an active volcano and part of the Teng-ger mas-sif in East Java, Indonesia.

Coal transportation by truck, Russia, Kuzbass, extractive industry

CARBON ECONOMY AND CLIMATE CHANGE

The main cause of global warming, beyond what the Earth naturally does, is human activity. There are more humans alive on Earth than ever before, and all of them are actively doing things. A lot of the things they do generate both heat and pollution.

The good thing for us is all the power the fossil fuels have provided. Fossil fuels power factories and hospitals, cars and airplanes. Until recently, almost all the electricity we used was created by burning coal.

Burning fossil fuel generates pollution that slowly builds up in the atmosphere. The pollution in the atmosphere acts like a great big sweater over the whole Earth, keeping more of Earth's natural heat, and the heat all our activity and fuel-burning causes, from escaping into space.

And so our Earth is getting steadily warmer, and much faster than almost anybody expected.

A coal powered power station at dusk.

An ice core segment extracted from an aquifer with trapped water collecting at the lower left of the core.

STUDYING CLIMATE CHANGE

Weather records, in terms of people writing down what was happening each day where they were, only go back a bit over a hundred years, so scientists have to look elsewhere to understand Earth's climate over centuries and longer periods of time.

One tool they use is ice bubbles!

At the North and South Poles, layer upon layer of ice has built up, and the lowest layers are from hundreds and thousands of years ago. In those layer are tiny bubbles of air. Those bubbles are a witness to what the air was like when that layer of ice formed, and so tell us about the climate in past times.

A sliver of Antarctic ice revealing the myriad enclosed tiny bubbles of air. Air bubbles trapped in ice hundreds or even thousands of years ago are providing vital information about past levels of greenhouse gases in the Earth's atmosphere.

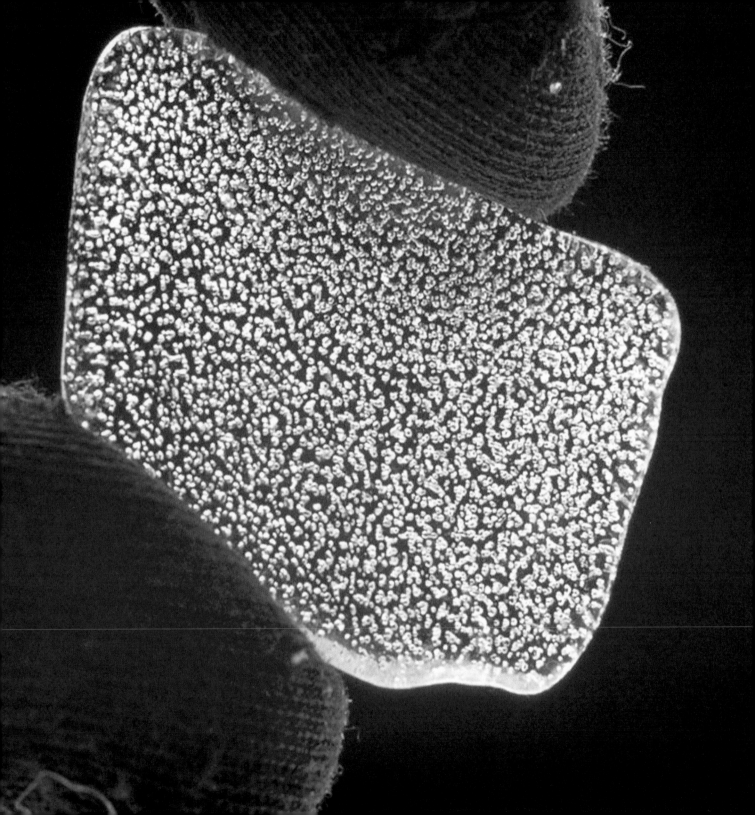

Scientists bore long, narrow holes down into the ice and bring up core samples of ice from our distant past. They can then see how much carbon dioxide was in the air, what pollen was floating about, and what other chemicals were present.

National Ice Core Laboratory (NICL) provides safe and secure storage and curation of ice cores recovered by researchers from the Earth's Polar Regions.

The scenic Sossusvlei and Deadvlei, clay and salt pan with braided Acacia trees surrounded by majestic sand dunes. Namib Naukluft National Park.

IS IT TRUE?

Although almost every competent scientist agrees that the Earth is rapidly warming, and that human activity is largely causing it, some scientists disagree. Some argue that the warming is part of a natural cycle, and that rather than trying to slow it down we should just learn to live on a warmer planet.

Those who believe that human activity is causing rapid global warming and climate change say, *Let's do both! Let's figure out how to live in a warmer world and at the same time slow down causing the warming.* The reason for this is that global warming, now that it is started, will continue increasing, only at a much slower rate, if we stopped burning all fossil fuels tomorrow.

A field suffering drought.

Hanoi skyline cityscape at twilight period. Air pollution in the big city.

EFFECTS
OF CLIMATE
CHANGE

Climate change will not be the same everywhere. Some places will get just a little warmer, while others will get so much hotter that it will be hard for humans to continue living there. A very few places might get colder.

But what will be true almost everywhere is that the climate will become less predictable. Our weather, day to day, week to week, and year to year, will get more erratic and more extreme. Some places will get in a week the rainfall they used to expect in a whole year, and other places may see a long period with no rainfall at all.

ECOSYSTEMS UNDER THREAT

You can divide the Earth into many ecosystems— the cold, dry Arctic, the wet, warm rain forest, and so on. In each ecosystem there are animals and plants that have developed to live and thrive in the climate of that ecosystem.

Each ecosystem is balanced based on the traditional patterns of its climate, soil, available water, and so on. What happens when that balance gets thrown off? What happens when the polar bears can't find ice floes to stand on, because global warming has caused almost all the Arctic ice to melt away? What happens to young plants when, instead of growing in a mild spring, they have to try to survive under lashing rain and gale-force winds?

And each piece in the ecosystem is related to other pieces. If certain plants don't grow, certain animals and insects don't have the food they are expecting at the time they need it. If those animals die, then the predators that rely on them will have nothing to eat; the insects that die are not available to pollinate plants so the next crops of plants can grow.

Bee death.

Disrupting an ecosystem does not just mean trouble for us humans, who might go to our favorite vacation place and find it is not like it used to be in past summers. It may mean the whole ecosystem will collapse. Many plant and animal species will become extinct in that area, or even throughout the whole world.

Oil spill - pollution - ecological disaster.

Earth hour promotion campaign concept: Saving energy, efficiency.

HOW CAN WE STOP GLOBAL WARMING?

To slow and eventually reverse global warming, and to reduce the effects of climate change, we have to reduce human activities that make the planet hotter. The most obvious way of doing that is to move away from burning fossil fuels and adopt using renewable energy that does not cause the same damage to our ecosystems. We should also concentrate on making our machines and our lives more efficient, so we do more while burning less fuel and using up less of what our planet has available.

WHAT YOU CAN DO

There are all sorts of small steps you can take to reduce what you yourself contribute to global warming and climate change.

- Turn off lights, the television, and the air conditioner when you don't really need them.

- Walk or ride your bike, or take public transportation, rather than firing up the family car.

- Put on a sweater instead of turning up the heat.

At a larger level, your family or your town could look into installing solar panels or wind generators, and getting (and sharing) more energy from sunlight and wind than from burning coal and oil.

Aerial view of Solar panels Photovoltaic systems in Italy, industrial landscape.

There are big changes that only governments can make happen. But you can even help with that! Find out who your elected representatives are at the local, state, and national level. Write them, call them, or visit them in person and ask what they are doing to help slow global warming and reduce climate change.

Young pine saplings in field.

Humidity

Temperature Over Oceans

Sea Surface Temperature

Sea Ice

Sea L

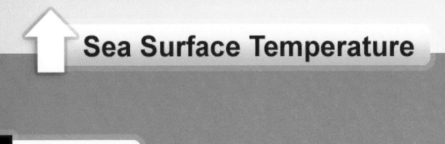

Ocean Heat Content

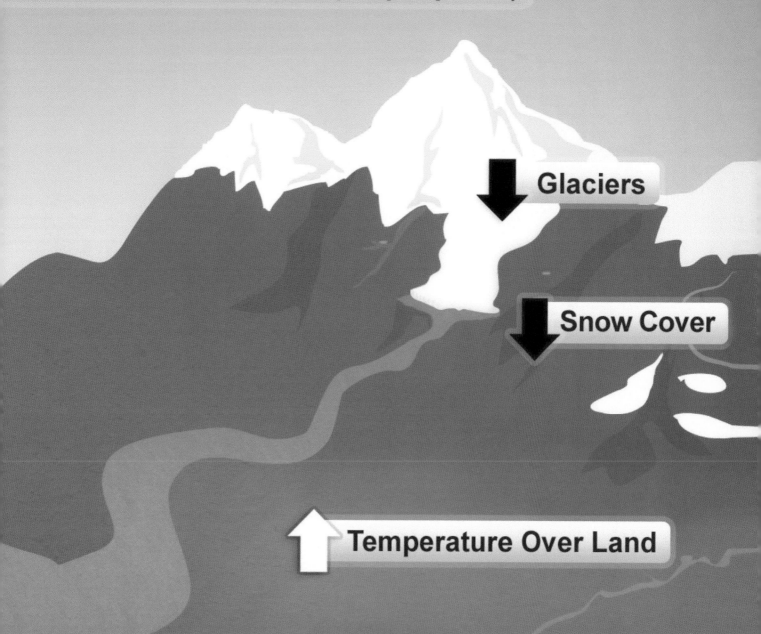

Warming World

Temperature Near Surface (Troposphere)

Glaciers

Snow Cover

Temperature Over Land

One person asking a politician to act will not get far. If a hundred thousand people ask the politician to act, he or she will take notice!

LEARN MORE ABOUT THE EARTH

Learn more about this wonderful Earth we live on in Baby Professor books like *Top 100 Interesting Earth Facts for Kids* and *Peeling the Earth like an Onion.*

Printed in Great Britain
by Amazon